READERS FOR TEENS

The Fishermen's Village

Luiz H. Rose

Maiza Fatureto

Tereza Sekiya

Series coordinator
Sérgio Varela

CAMBRIDGE
UNIVERSITY PRESS

University Printing House, Cambridge CB2 8BS, United Kingdom

One Liberty Plaza, 20th Floor, New York, NY 10006, USA

477 Williamstown Road, Port Melbourne, VIC 3207, Australia

314–321, 3rd Floor, Plot 3, Splendor Forum, Jasola District Centre, New Delhi – 110025, India

103 Penang Road, #05-06/07, Visioncrest Commercial, Singapore 238467

Cambridge University Press is part of the University of Cambridge.

It furthers the University's mission by disseminating knowledge in the pursuit of education, learning and research at the highest international levels of excellence.

www.cambridge.org

© Cambridge University Press 2008

This publication is in copyright. Subject to statutory exception and to the provisions of relevant collective licensing agreements, no reproduction of any part may take place without the written permission of Cambridge University Press.

First published 2008

20 19 18 17 16 15 14 13 12 11 10 9

Printed in Great Britain by CPI Group (UK) Ltd, Croydon CR0 4YY

A catalogue record for this publication is available from the British Library

ISBN 978-0-521-72141-7 paperback

Cambridge University Press has no responsibility for the persistence or accuracy of URLs for external or third-party internet websites referred to in this publication, and does not guarantee that any content on such websites is, or will remain, accurate or appropriate.

Illustrations by *Fábio Moon*

Art direction, book design and layout services: A+ Comunicação, Brazil

Contents

Chapter 1
New friends   5

Chapter 2
A big problem   7

Chapter 3
The idea   10

Chapter 4
The newspaper article   14

Chapter 5
The meeting   17

Chapter 6
A continuous fight   20

Chapter 1
New friends

Mai lives in a small town near the ocean. She's 13 and she lives with her mother and father in a small house.

Mai's mother is a housewife and her father is a fisherman. Mai's father has a small boat. He goes fishing every day with two other men.

Mai loves school. Her favorite subjects are biology and history. Mai is always telling her family and friends that she wants to study fish when she gets older.

When she isn't at school, Mai loves to walk along the beach and look at the different seashells and fish. One day, while Mai was walking along the beach, she saw an older woman fishing. When Mai got closer to the woman, they started to talk to each other.

Mai learned that the woman was from a big

city and that she was at the beach on vacation. She didn't work anymore, but she was a doctor when she was younger. Her name was Amy Young, but everybody called her Dr. Young.

Mai and Dr. Young talked to each other a lot that day. They talked about a lot of different things, but they both had one thing they liked to talk about the most – nature.

Mai told Dr. Young a lot of things about the seashells and fish in that area. Dr. Young listened carefully to Mai.

Dr. Young told Mai many interesting stories about nature, too. Mai enjoyed listening to her. Mai was happy to have a new friend.

Chapter 2
A big problem

When Mai got home, she noticed that her mother was crying.

"What's the matter, Mom?" Mai asked.

"I think your father will have to sell his boat. He isn't catching enough fish to make money anymore," Mai's mother answered.

"Why is that?" asked Mai.

"Sit down and I will tell you everything," said Mai's mother.

"It all started about five years ago when the new factory opened in town. Since then, there are fewer and fewer fish and your father has to go farther and farther away to catch them," Mai's mother explained.

"Is the factory responsible for that?" Mai asked.

"I think so. They throw a lot of trash in the ocean. The trash is probably killing the fish," her mother answered.

That night, Mai couldn't sleep very well. She kept thinking about the problem of the fish. She wanted to do something about it, but what could she do?

Chapter 3
The idea

The next day, Mai saw Dr. Young at the beach again after school. Dr. Young noticed that Mai was worried.

"What's wrong, Mai? You look worried," she asked.

Mai explained her father's problem. She also told Dr. Young about the trash from the factory. Dr. Young listened carefully to Mai's story.

"Did your father or mother talk to other people in the town about this problem?" Dr. Young asked.

"Yes, they did, but no one knows what to do," Mai answered.

"Did they try to talk to people at the factory about it?" asked Dr. Young.

"Yes, they did. They talked to them. The people at the factory said they would look at the problem, but they didn't do anything about it," Mai explained.

"Well, I have an idea," Dr. Young says.

"Really? What is it?" asked Mai.

"You should write a letter to the factory from the town and ask everybody to sign it. Then send the letter to the factory and to the newspaper," suggested Dr. Young.

"That's an excellent idea. Can you help me write the letter?" Mai asked.

"Sure, let's go to your house and I will talk to your father and your mother about it," said Dr. Young.

Dr. Young went to Mai's house with her. When they got there, Dr. Young explained her idea to Mai's parents. They really liked the idea. They all helped Mai write the letter.

The next day, Mai made copies of the letter and asked all her friends to help her find people to sign them.

A week later, Mai went to the post office to mail copies of the letters to the factory and to the newspaper.

Chapter 4
The newspaper article

A few days later, the newspaper reporter in Mai's town met with Mai and some other people in the town. He wanted to learn more about the problem with the trash from the factory.

He spoke to a lot of people and took a lot of photos, including photos of Mai, Mai's parents, and Dr. Young.

One week later, while Mai was walking near the newsstand, the man working at the newsstand asked her, "Did you see your picture in the newspaper today?"

"My picture? No, I didn't. Are you sure it's me?"

"Yes, I'm sure. Take a look," he said.

Mai opened the newspaper quickly. When she saw her picture she smiled and started to read the article.

In the article, the reporter told the story of the problems the fishermen were having. He also talked about the trash from the factory that was probably causing the problem.

Mai was very excited. She ran to Dr. Young to show her the article.

Dr. Young was very happy for Mai. She hoped that the people at the factory would now do something about the problem.

Chapter 5
The meeting

A few days later, Mr. Stewart, the manager of the factory, asked the people of the town to have a meeting.

"Our factory is worried about the community and the environment. We want to help," said Mr. Stewart at the beginning of the meeting.

"We're going to change the way we throw trash out from the factory right away. We hope that this will help make the ocean cleaner," he said.

"We also want to help the community. We will give computers to the school and an ambulance to the town's hospital," Mr. Stewart added.

The people of the town listened carefully to Mr. Stewart. They listened to his promises, but they didn't believe him very much.

The same day, the factory started to throw out trash in a better way. They didn't throw any of it in the ocean. They threw all of the trash in big trash cans.

Two weeks later, when Mai arrived at school, all the students were very excited. They had new computers. The factory sent them.

The town hospital also received a new ambulance.

But the situation for Mai's father didn't get any better. He still couldn't catch many fish.

Mai talked to Dr. Young about it.

"Do you think it will take a long time for the ocean to recover from the trash?" Mai asked.

"I have no idea. Nature is usually quick to recover from damage, if the damage isn't too bad. Let's hope for the best," Dr. Young said.

Mai went home and told her father what Dr. Young said. Mai's father decided that he wouldn't sell the boat. He decided to wait a few more months to see. Maybe things would get better.

Chapter 6
A continuous fight

The day came for Dr. Young to go back to her city. Mai was sad because she was going to miss her new friend. Dr. Young was sad, too. She promised to return the next year.

Mai gave Dr. Young a little present. She gave Dr. Young a beautiful seashell. Dr. Young also gave Mai a present. She gave Mai a small camera and asked her to take photos of nature.

"When I come back, I want to see your photos," Dr. Young said.

"Sure. I am going to take lots of photos and show them to you," Mai said.

About six months after Dr. Young left, the fish started to come back to the ocean near the town. Fortunately, the damage to the ocean could be stopped!

Mai could now enjoy her walks along the beach again without worrying about the trash from the factory. It would take several years for the ocean to get completely better, but Mai was happy it was getting better already.

One day, Mai was at school reading the news on the Internet. She read an article about a problem with people throwing trash in the ocean in a town in South America.

Mai decided to write to the people of the town immediately. They wrote back to Mai and they started to exchange e-mails. Mai tried to help them, and she gave them many ideas. Mai was very happy she could help other people.

Mai's fight to keep the oceans clean continued.